Grade 1

by Janet Cain

Carson-Dellosa Publishing LLC
Greensboro, North Carolina

Credits

Content Editor: Amy Gamble

Copy Editor: Karen Seberg

Layout and Cover Design: Lori Jackson

 This book has been correlated to state, common core state, national, and Canadian provincial standards. Visit *www.carsondellosa.com* to search for and view its correlations to your standards.

Carson-Dellosa Publishing LLC
PO Box 35665
Greensboro, NC 27425 USA

ISBN 978-1-936024-17-9
335101151

Table of Contents

Skills Matrix

	Counting and Estimating	Ordinal Numbers	Addition	Subtraction	Multiplication	Division	Place Value	Problem Solving	Patterns	Number Relationships	Measurement	Time	Geometry	Data Analysis and Probability	Sorting and Classifying	Algebra	Fractions	Money
6	★		★				★											
7	★	★							★	★								
8	★		★	★						★								
9	★			★			★											
10			★	★						★							★	
11	★	★					★											★
12	★		★						★									★
13			★	★			★			★							★	
14	★		★	★	★		★											
15	★		★	★	★					★								★
16	★		★		★					★								
17	★		★						★	★						★		
18	★		★						★	★						★		
19			★	★					★	★						★		
20			★							★						★		
21			★	★			★		★					★		★		
22	★			★			★		★	★						★		
23				★					★	★	★				★	★		
24	★								★						★	★		
25	★			★					★		★					★		
26	★		★	★				★	★				★			★		
27	★		★	★			★		★				★		★	★		
28													★					
29													★					
30													★		★			
31													★		★			
32													★					
33													★		★			
34													★		★			
35													★					
36													★					
37								★					★					
38								★								★		
39	★										★	★						
40											★	★			★			
41											★	★						
42											★	★					★	
43											★	★			★			
44											★	★						
45											★	★				★	★	
46										★	★					★	★	
47											★	★	★					
48	★										★	★					★	
49	★										★	★						
50	★													★	★			
51	★													★				
52	★													★				
53	★													★				
54	★													★				
55	★													★				
56	★													★				
57	★													★				
58	★													★				
59														★	★			
60														★	★			

Introduction

Problem solving is a critical skill for understanding and applying math concepts. *Thinking Kids'™ Math Analogies* provides students with ample problem-solving practice for thinking analogically while reinforcing standards-based math skills. Analogies build conceptual bridges between what is familiar and what is new.

Thinking Kids'™ Math Analogies contains five sections, one for each content strand of the National Council of Teachers of Mathematics (NCTM) standards: Number and Operations, Algebra, Geometry, Measurement, and Data Analysis and Probability. These sections are ordered by difficulty to build skills and allow for differentiation. The level is indicated by a code at the bottom of each page.

★   Basic: equivalency-based analogies and beginning skills

★ ★   Intermediate: part equivalency-based and part logic-based analogies with more difficult skills

★ ★ ★ Advanced: logic-based analogies with challenging skills

Before students work with the analogies in this book, they will need to be familiar with the format of an analogy and the proper way to read and interpret analogies. You may wish to give students practice with a few simple verbal analogies, such as "*up* is to *down* as *on* is to *off*," before modeling math analogies. Teach students to read an analogy as this:

$$A \underset{\text{is to}}{:} B \underset{\text{as}}{::} C \underset{\text{is to}}{:} D$$

Determine the connection or relationship between A and B on the left side of the double colon (::). Apply that same connection to find the missing item (D) on the right and to complete the analogy.

Solving mathematical analogies can help students understand mathematical relationships and vocabulary. The *How do you know?* component asks students to write how they solved the analogy. Students should be encouraged to use mathematical vocabulary to explain their thinking.

As students progress through the book, they will not only gain an understanding of analogies but also build a solid mathematics foundation for their future.

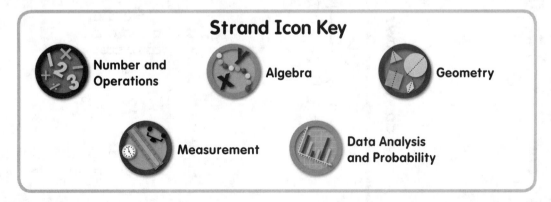

Strand Icon Key

Number and Operations

Algebra

Geometry

Measurement

Data Analysis and Probability

Name ANDREA

Date _____

Complete each analogy and explain your answer.

1 one : :·: :: five :

How do you know?

2

1 2 3 4 5 6 7 8 9 10

: 1 + 4 = 5 ::

1 2 3 4 5 6 7 8 9 10

: ·.·:

How do you know?

3 :::: : 12 ::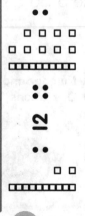

How do you know?

Name ANDREA   Date _____

Complete each analogy and explain your answer.

1 [birds image] : five, :: [birds image] : ITEN.

How do you know? _____
BECASUS ICMOTIT

2 1, 2, 3, 4, 5 : 4 :: 11, 12, 13, __, 14, 15 : 13

How do you know? _____
BECASUS ICMOTIT

3 [cars image with arrow] : third :: [cars image with arrow] : FIRST ~~KNOW~~

How do you know? _____
BECASUS IKNOW

Name _____

Complete each analogy and explain your answer.

1 60 + 1 : 61 :: 10 + 1 :: _1_

How do you know? _____

2 one less than 23 : 22 :: one less than 15 : _14_

How do you know? _____

3

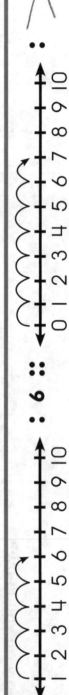

: 6 :: _7_

How do you know? _____

How do you know? _____

Name _____ Date _____

Complete each analogy and explain your answer.

1

: 8 :: : 3

How do you know?

_____

2 59 : 5 tens, 9 ones :: 12 : ITEN : 2 ONES

How do you know?

_____

3  : 3 ::  : 4

BECASUS I COUT

How do you know?

_____

Number and Operations

9

Name ANDREA   Date _____

Complete each analogy and explain your answer.

1 [fraction bar 1/2] :: $\frac{1}{2}$ :: [fraction bar 1/4] :

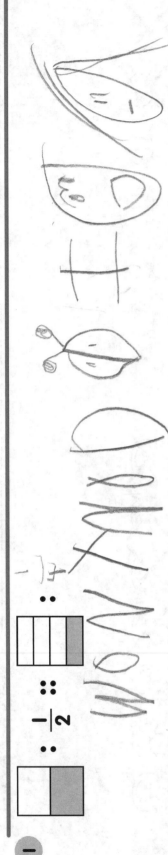

How do you know?
_____

2 27 [circled] : 54 :: < :: 60 (>) 56 :

How do you know?
_____

3 2 + 3 : 5 :: 5 − 3 : 2

How do you know?
_____

Name _____ Date _____

Complete each analogy and explain your answer.

1.     5¢ 5¢ 5¢ : 15¢ :: 10¢ 10¢ 10¢ : 30¢

How do you know? _____

2. fourth, _FIF_ , sixth : fifth :: first, ___ , third :: 11

How do you know? _____

3.  4 tens, 6 ones : 46 :: 2 tens, 3 ones : 23

How do you know? _____

Number and Operations

★★ · © Carson-Dellosa

11

Name _____

Date _____

Complete each analogy and explain your answer.

1 9 + 4 + 5 : 18 :: 2 + 6 + 7 : 15

How do you know? _____

2 (10¢) : 5¢ 5¢ :: 5¢ :

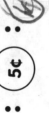

How do you know? _____

3 12, 11, 10, 9 : 9 :: 20, 19, 18, 17 : 17

How do you know? _____

Name _____

Date _____

Complete each analogy and explain your answer.

1 $75 + \boxed{|||||||||} : 85 :: 35 + \boxed{|||||||||} :: \boxed{45}$

How do you know? _____

2 $9 + 9 : 18 :: 9 - 9 :: \boxed{0}$

How do you know? _____

3 🐞🐞🐝 : $\frac{1}{3}$ :: 🐞🐞🐞🐝 : $\frac{1}{4}$

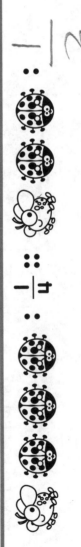

How do you know? _____

Number and Operations

13

Name ANDREX Date _____

Complete each analogy and explain your answer.

1    : 2 + 2 + 2 + 2 :: 8 : 2+2 :3 :6

How do you know? _____

2   6 [/] 3 = 3 : − :: 12 [+] 5 = 17 : _____

How do you know? _____

3   95 : 90 + 5 :: 73 : 70 + 3

How do you know? _____

Number and Operations   14   ★★★ • © Carson-Dellosa

Name _____ Date _____

Complete each analogy and explain your answer.

1  : 25 ::  : 16

2 78 | 79 | 80 : 79 :: 39 | 40 | 41 : 40

How do you know? _____

3 5¢ 1¢ 1¢ 1¢ 1¢ : 10¢ :: 10¢ 10¢ 5¢ : 25¢

How do you know? _____

How do you know? _____

Name _AMREA_

Date _____

Complete each analogy and explain your answer.

1 37 : 27 and 47 :: 58 :

58 : 37 > 27 / 27 / 27 /

48 = 68

How do you know?

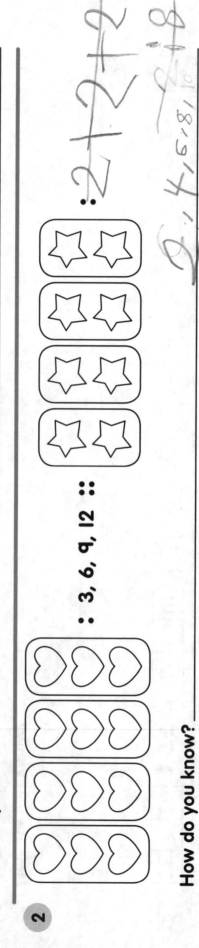

2 :: 3, 6, 9, 12 ::

: 27 / 2 / 2 / 2 /

2, 4, 6, 8, 10

How do you know?

3 make 10 from 7 : add 3 :: make 10 from 6 :

add 4

How do you know?

Number and Operations

16

Name _____   Date _____

Complete each analogy and explain your answer.

1   $\square$ $\triangle$ $\square$ $\triangle$ $\square$: $\square$ :: $\bigcirc$ $\bigcirc$ $\square$ $\bigcirc$ $\square$: $\bigcirc$

How do you know? _____

2   $7 + 3 = 10$: $3 + 7 = 10$ :: $6 + 2 = 8$: $2 + 6 = $

How do you know? _____

3   $20, 30, 40, 50$: 50 :: $60, 70, 80, 90$: 90

How do you know? _____

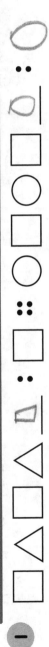

Name _AMIREA_ Date _____

Complete each analogy and explain your answer.

1 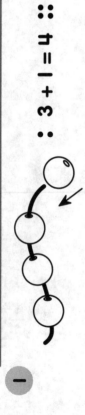 : 3 + 1 = 4 ::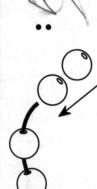

How do you know? _____

2 12 + 0 : 12 :: 49 + 0 : 49

How do you know? _____

3 1, 3, 5, 7, 9, 11 : 11 :: 2, 4, 6, 8, 10, 12 : 12

How do you know? _____

Algebra   18

Name _____ Date _____

Complete each analogy and explain your answer.

1 3 + 4 = 7 : 4 + 3 = 7 :: 6 + 5 = 11 : 5 + 6 = 11

How do you know? _____

2 25, 30, 35, 40, 45 : 45 :: 60, 65, 70, 75, 80 : 80

How do you know? _____

3  : 6 − 3 = 3 ::  : 5 − 2 = 3

How do you know? _____

Name __ANDREA__   Date __THRN__

Complete each analogy and explain your answer.

1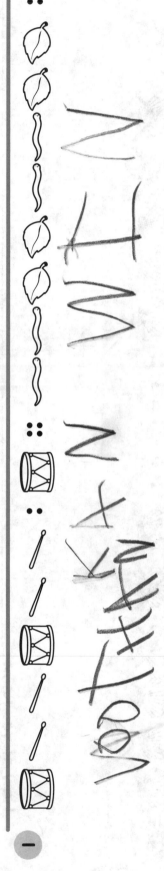

N I I N

K A N   W I N

V00 K K N

How do you know?
_____

2   $2 + \boxed{|} = 3 : |$ :: $7 + \boxed{\triangle} = 9 :$ ::

How do you know?
_____

3   ABCDABCDA __B__ : B :: XYZXYZX __Y__ :

How do you know?
_____

How do you know?
_____

Name _____   Date _____

Complete each analogy and explain your answer.

1   ⬜ ⬜ ⬜ ▢ :: ◯ ◯ ◯ ◦

How do you know? _____

2   20 + ⬜ = 70 : 50 :: 40 + ⬜ = 60 :

How do you know? _____

3   10 – 2 : 8 :: 10 – 8 : 5

How do you know? _____

How do you know? _____

Name _____ Date 10/22/[crossed out]/2017   10-22-20

Complete each analogy and explain your answer.

1   40 − [30] = 10 : 30 :: 80 − [80] = 10 : 80

How do you know?

I SOW THA NUMBR

2   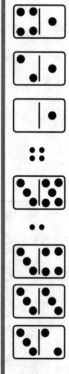   :: ∷

How do you know?

3   12, 18, 96, 84 : even :: 75, 11, 63, 99 : ODD

How do you know?

How do you know?

Name _____ Date _____

Complete each analogy and explain your answer.

1

| 1 | 2 | 3 | 4 | 5 | 6 | 7 | 8 | 9 | 10 | : 8 :: | 31 | 32 | 33 | 34 | 35 | 36 | 37 | 38 | 39 | 40 | : 38 |

2

 : time :: $1¢$ $10¢$ $1 : MONEY

How do you know? _____

3

Ana's Growth Chart

38
37
36

: 2 inches ::

Greg's Growth Chart

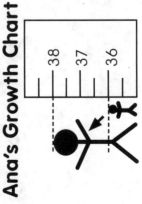

42
41
40

: 4 INCHES INCH

How do you know? _____

How do you know? _____

Algebra   23

★★ · © Carson-Dellosa

Name _____

Date _____

Complete each analogy and explain your answer.

1 6, 8, 10, _____, 14 : 12 :: 16, 18, 20, _____, 24 :

How do you know? _____

_____

2  : plants ::  :

How do you know? _____

_____

3

Month	Money in Tia's Bank
January	50 cents
February	60 cents
March	75 cents

: more money each month ::

Month	Nathan's Marbles
January	20 marbles
February	15 marbles
March	12 marbles

::

How do you know? _____

_____

Name _____   Date _____

Complete each analogy and explain your answer.

1   3, 6, 9, _____, 15 : 12 :: 4, 8, 12, _____, 20 :

How do you know? _____

2
2 inches — 5 inches — : 3 inches :: 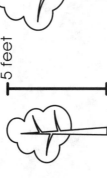 5 feet —  7 feet — :

How do you know? _____

3   ABCABCA : ABC :: DDFFDDFFD :

How do you know? _____

Name _____ Date _____

Complete each analogy and explain your answer.

1  : ABAB :: : _____

How do you know? _____

2 124, 126, 128, 130, ... : add 2 :: 113, 116, 119, 122, ... : _____

How do you know? _____

3

Name	Age
Julie	10
Matt	1 year older than Julie

:: :: = :: ::

Name	Age
Rosa	5 years younger than Dave
Dave	13

How do you know? _____

Name _____   Date _____

Complete each analogy and explain your answer.

1 29, 27, 25, 23, . . . : subtract 2 :: 50, 45, 40, 35, . . . : _____

How do you know? _____

2 2 + 2, 3 + 3, 4 + 4, 5 + 5, ____ : 6 + 6 :: 1 – 1, 2 – 2, 3 – 3, 4 – 4, ____ : _____

How do you know? _____

3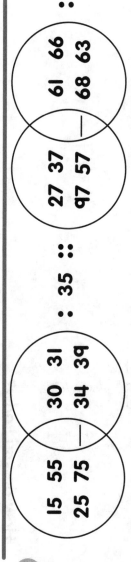

     : 35 ::

15	55	30	31
25	75	34	39

27	37	61	66
97	57	68	63

    : _____

How do you know? _____

How do you know? _____

Name _____ Date _____

Complete each analogy and explain your answer.

1   rectangle : [ ] :: circle : _____

How do you know? _____

2   triangle : 3 corners :: rectangle : _____

How do you know? _____

3    : sphere :: _____

How do you know? _____

Name _____ Date _____

Complete each analogy and explain your answer.

1 triangle :  :: square : _____

How do you know? _____

2 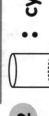 : cylinder ::  : _____

How do you know? _____

3 ⬠ : 5 sides :: ▭ : _____

How do you know? _____

Name _____ Date _____

Complete each analogy and explain your answer.

1  : rectangle :: : _____

How do you know? _____

2   : octagon :: : _____

How do you know? _____

3  : triangles :: _____

How do you know? _____

Geometry   30   ★ • • © Carson-Dellosa

Name _____ Date _____

Complete each analogy and explain your answer.

1. ○ △ △ ○ : △ :: △ △ □ △ : :

How do you know? _____

2. 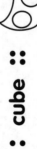 : cube ::  : :

How do you know? _____

3. 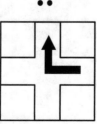 : Turn right. :: 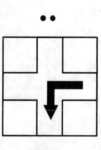 : :

How do you know? _____

Geometry

31

Name _____

Date _____

Complete each analogy and explain your answer.

1 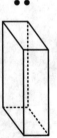 : squares ::  : _____

_____

How do you know? _____

2  : 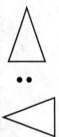 ::  : _____

_____

How do you know? _____

3  : 3 equal sides ::  : _____

_____

How do you know? _____

Name _____ Date _____

Complete each analogy and explain your answer.

1 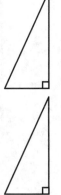 ::

How do you know? _____

2  ::

How do you know? _____

3 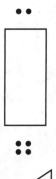 ::

How do you know? _____

How do you know? _____

Name _____ Date _____

Complete each analogy and explain your answer.

1.    : left ::  : ..

How do you know? _____

2.  ::  : ..

How do you know? _____

3. 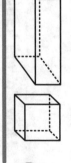  ::  : ..

How do you know? _____

How do you know? _____

Name _____ Date _____

Complete each analogy and explain your answer.

1  **::**

_____

How do you know? _____

2 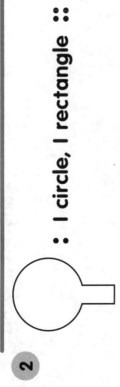 **: 1 circle, 1 rectangle :: ____ : ____**

_____

How do you know? _____

3 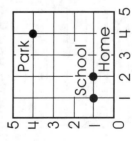 **school : near home :: park : ____**

_____

How do you know? _____

Name _____

Date _____

Complete each analogy and explain your answer.

1

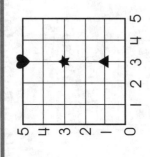

heart : above star :: triangle : _____

How do you know? _____

_____

2

_____

How do you know? _____

_____

3

 : closed figure :: ⟍△ : _____

How do you know? _____

_____

★★★ • © Carson-Dellosa

Name _____ Date _____

Complete each analogy and explain your answer.

1. 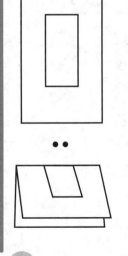 ::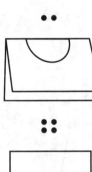

_____

How do you know?

_____

2.  : 5 triangles ::

_____

How do you know?

_____

3. 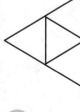 ::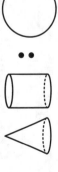

_____

How do you know?

_____

★★★ · © Carson-Dellosa

Geometry   37

Name _____

Date _____

Complete each analogy and explain your answer.

1

How do you know? _____

2
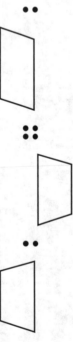

How do you know? _____

3
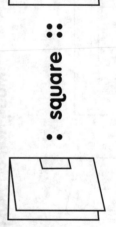

: square ::

How do you know? _____

Name _____ Date _____

Complete each analogy and explain your answer.

1 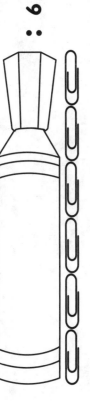 :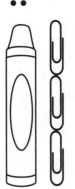

:: 6 paper clips :: ▪▪

How do you know? _____

2 1 o'clock :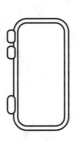

:: half past 7 o'clock :  ▪

How do you know? _____

3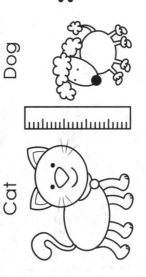

Alex   Tia

: Tia is taller. ::

Cat   Dog  ▪▪

How do you know? _____

Name _____ Date _____

Complete each analogy and explain your answer.

1.  : tallest to shortest ::  : _____

How do you know? _____

2.  : four o'clock ::  : _____

How do you know? _____

3. 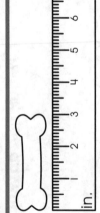 : _____ ::  : 3 inches : _____

How do you know? _____

Measurement

40

Complete each analogy and explain your answer.

1  :  :: The watermelon is heavier. ::

How do you know? _____

2  :  :: hour hand :: _____

How do you know? _____

3 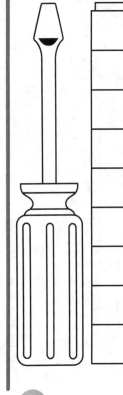 : : q cubes :: _____

How do you know? _____

Name _____

Date _____

Complete each analogy and explain your answer.

1
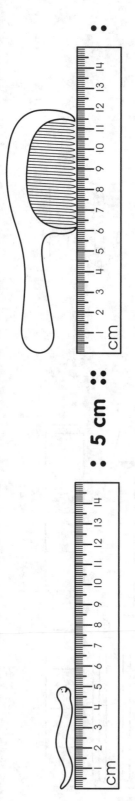

: 5 cm :: _____

How do you know? _____

2 spring : summer :: autumn : _____

How do you know? _____

3
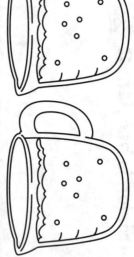
: 1 cup ::
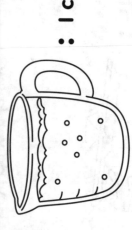
_____

How do you know? _____

Name _____ Date _____

Complete each analogy and explain your answer.

1

 9:00 A.M. :  10:30 A.M. ::  7:30 A.M. :  10:00 P.M. : 8:30 P.M. : 11:30 P.M. :: __

How do you know? _____

2

  :: < :: 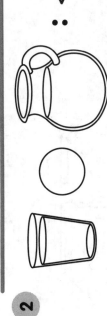  __

How do you know? _____

3

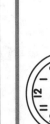 : weight ::  __

How do you know? _____

Name _____

Date _____

Complete each analogy and explain your answer.

1   [6:30 A.M.] [8:00 A.M.] : [11:30 A.M.] :: [8:00 P.M.] [9:30 P.M.] [6:30 P.M.] :

How do you know? _____

2    : books ::  :

How do you know? _____

3    : measuring cup :: ⟶ :

How do you know? _____

Name _____ Date _____

Complete each analogy and explain your answer.

1

   : 1 centimeter ::  :

How do you know? _____

2

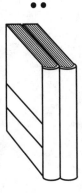 : 2 pounds :: 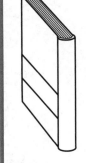  :

How do you know? _____

3 grams, ounces, hours, pounds : hours :: yards, cups, inches, feet :

How do you know? _____

Measurement

45

Name _____

Date _____

Complete each analogy and explain your answer.

1

String A   String B   ∴ **B** ∷   Ribbon A   Ribbon B ∴

How do you know?

_____

2

⬭ ∷ I gram ∷   ∴

_____

How do you know?

_____

3

∷ length ∷    ∴

_____

How do you know?

_____

Name _____ Date _____

Complete each analogy and explain your answer.

1   fox   cow   fox   mouse   fish   whale   fish   clam

   :: mouse, fox, cow :: __ __ __

How do you know? _____

2

A

B

:: A :: __

C

D

How do you know? _____

3

March

Sun.	Mon.	Tues.	Wed.	Thur.	Fri.	Sat.
			1	2	3	4
5	6	7	8	⑮ wait		
5	6	7	8	9	⑩	11
12	13	14	⑮	16	17	18
19	20	21	22	23	24	25
26	27	28	29	30	31	

: 5 days :: __

June

Sun.	Mon.	Tues.	Wed.	Thur.	Fri.	Sat.
		1	2	3	4	5
6	7	8	9	10	11	12
13	14	15	16	17	18	19
20	㉑	22	23	24	25	26
27	㉘	29	30			

How do you know? _____

Name _____

Date _____

Complete each analogy and explain your answer.

1  : 1 pound :: 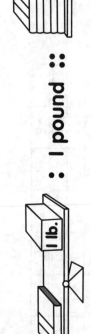 : ? __

How do you know? _____

2 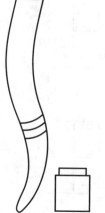 : about 5 cubes :: 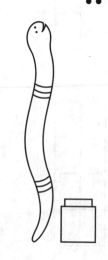 : __

How do you know? _____

3  : 30 minutes :: : __

How do you know? _____

Measurement

48

Name _____

Date _____

Complete each analogy and explain your answer.

1

 : about 5 paper clips :: 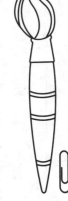 : _____

How do you know? _____

2 April 13 : yesterday :: April 15 : _____

How do you know? _____

3

 : one hour ::  : _____

How do you know? _____

Measurement

49

Name _____ Date _____

Complete each analogy and explain your answer.

1 5 crayons : ≢ :: 16 crayons : _____

How do you know? _____

2

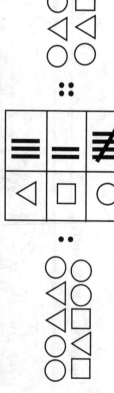

How do you know? _____

3

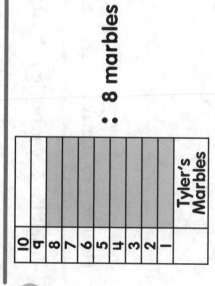

:: 8 marbles :: _____

How do you know? _____

Data Analysis and Probability

50

★ · © Carson-Dellosa

Name _____ Date _____

Complete each analogy and explain your answer.

1  baseballs : 12 baseballs ::  baseball bats : _____ : : ____

baseballs
0 1 2 3 4 5 6 7 8 9 10 11 12

baseball bats
0 1 2 3 4 5 6 7 8 9 10 11 12

How do you know? _____

2 2 : 1 :: A : B : _____ : : ____

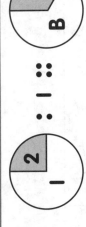

How do you know? _____

3 balloons : 7 balloons :: party hats : ____

How do you know? _____

Name _____ Date _____

Complete each analogy and explain your answer.

1

	5
	4
	3
	2
	1
△	

∴

△ △ △

∴

	5
	4
	3
	2
	1
□	

∴

How do you know? _____

2

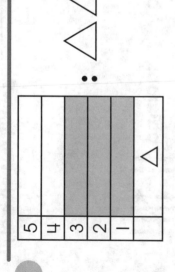

∷ 6 chickens ∷

∴

How do you know? _____

3

ponies	卌 卌 卌

∷ 15 ponies ∷

horses	卌 卌 卌 =

∴

How do you know? _____

How do you know? _____

Data Analysis and Probability

52

★ · © Carson-Dellosa

Name _____ Date _____

Complete each analogy and explain your answer.

1.

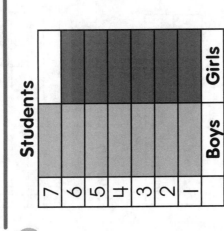

lemons : ⧸⧸⧸⧸⧸⧸ :: oranges : _____

How do you know? _____

2.

Students

7						
6						
5						
4						
3						
2						
1						
	Boys				**Girls**	

Girls : less :: Boys : _____

How do you know? _____

3.

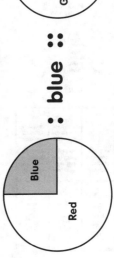

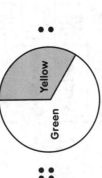

_____ : blue :: _____ :

How do you know? _____

Name _____ Date _____

Complete each analogy and explain your answer.

1

Favorite Color

Yellow	₦₦
Blue	₦₦ ₦₦
Red	₦₦ |||

_____ : Blue :: _____ : _____

Favorite Fruit

Oranges					
Grapes	₦₦			
Cherries				
Apples	₦₦				

How do you know?

2

January : 2 snowy days :: December : _____

Snowy Days

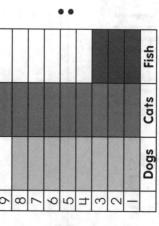

| December | ❄ ❄ ❄ ❄ ❄ |
| January | ❄ ❄ |

❄ = 1 snowy day

How do you know?

3

_____ : chickens :: _____ : _____

Farm Animals

9			
8			
7			
6			■
5			■
4		■	■
3	■	■	■
2	■	■	■
1	■	■	■
	Horses	Cows	Chickens

Pets

9			
8		■	
7		■	
6		■	
5		■	■
4	■	■	■
3	■	■	■
2	■	■	■
1	■	■	■
	Dogs	Cats	Fish

How do you know?

Data Analysis and Probability

54

★★ • © Carson-Dellosa

Name _____ Date _____

Complete each analogy and explain your answer.

1

Evan	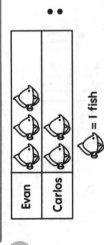
Carlos	

: Carlos ::

Nick	🖊🖊🖊🖊
Hunter	🖊

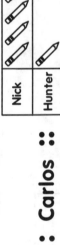 = 1 fish   🖊 = 1 pencil

How do you know? _____

2

Players on a Team

Football	😊😊😊😊😊😊😊😊
Baseball	😊😊😊😊
Soccer	😊😊😊😊😊😊😊😊

😊 = 1 player

: football and soccer ::

Competitors in a Race

Swimming	✓✓✓✓✓✓
Bicycling	✓✓✓✓✓✓✓✓✓✓✓✓
Horseback Riding	✓✓✓✓✓✓

✓ = 1 competitor

How do you know? _____

3

Toy Cars Sold

7			
6			
5			
4			
3			
2			
1			
	January	February	March

: March ::

Rainfall

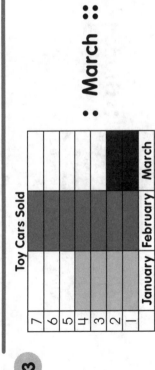

5			
4			
3			
2			
1			
	Monday	Tuesday	Friday

How do you know? _____

Name _____ Date _____

Complete each analogy and explain your answer.

1

Number of Classes

	Grade 1	Grade 2	Grade 3
7			■
6	■		■
5	■		■
4	■	■	■
3	■	■	■
2	■	■	■
1	■	■	■

: Grade 1 **::**

Number of Classes

	Grade 4	Grade 5	Grade 6
7			
6			
5			
4		■	■
3	■	■	■
2	■	■	■
1	■	■	■

::

How do you know? _____

2 You will find one million dollars today. **:** unlikely **::** You will eat lunch today. **:** _____

How do you know? _____

3

Favorite Juice

Grape Juice	卌 卌 ll
Orange Juice	卌
Apple Juice	卌 llll

: Grape Juice **::**

Favorite Place

Library	卌 卌
Park	卌 卌 l
Beach	卌 ll

::

How do you know? _____

Data Analysis and Probability

56

Name _____   Date _____

Complete each analogy and explain your answer.

1

Coins in My Pocket

	Dimes	Nickels	Pennies
6			
5			
4	▨		
3	▨	▨	
2	▨	▨	▧
1	▨	▨	▧

∷ 7 coins ∷

Coins in My Pocket

	Dimes	Nickels	Pennies
6			
5			
4			
3	▨		
2	▨		
1	▨	▨	▧

∷

How do you know? _____

2

Brown Snakes	𝍩 𝍩
Green Snakes	𝍩

∷ 15 snakes ∷

Large Birds	𝍩 ‖
Small Birds	𝍩 ‖

∷

How do you know? _____

3

Favorite Color	
Red	5
Blue	8
Green	3

∷ 16 votes ∷

Favorite Color	
Orange	1
Pink	3
Purple	6

∷

How do you know? _____

Name _____ Date _____

Complete each analogy and explain your answer.

1

Ways Our Class Gets to School		
Walk	✓✓✓✓✓	
Bus	✓✓✓✓✓✓✓✓✓	
Car	✓✓✓	

✓ = 1 student

5 : _____ :: the number of students who walk to school :: 10 : _____

How do you know?

_____

2

	Monday	Tuesday
77°		
76°		
75°		
74°		
73°	▓	
72°	▓	▓
71°	▓	▓
70°	▓	▓

_____ : down 2 degrees ::

	Wednesday	Thursday
81°		▓
80°		▓
79°		▓
78°		▓
77°		▓
76°		▓
75°	▓	▓
74°	▓	▓

_____

How do you know?

_____

3

You will pick a heart bead. : _____ :: certain :: You will pick a star bead. : _____

How do you know?

_____

Data Analysis and Probability

58

★★ • © Carson-Dellosa

Name _____ Date _____

Complete each analogy and explain your answer.

1

Recycling

Glass	♺ ♺ ♺
Paper	♺ ♺ ♺ ♺ ♺
Cans	♺

♺ = 1 pound

2 pounds : more paper than glass :: 3 pounds :

How do you know?

_____

2

Flowers	12
Trees	15
Bushes	9

: Plants ::

Blocks	21
Dolls	18
Stuffed Animals	35

:

How do you know?

_____

3

Berries

7			
6			
5			
4			
3			
2			
1			
	Blueberries	Cranberries	Strawberries

: strawberries, blueberries, cranberries ::

Flowers

7			
6			
5			
4			
3			
2			
1			
	Red	Yellow	Pink

:

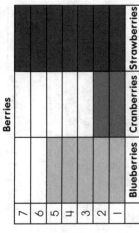

How do you know?

_____

★★ • © Carson-Dellosa

Name _____ Date _____

Complete each analogy and explain your answer.

1

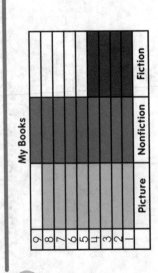

My Books		
9		
8		
7		
6		
5		
4		
3		
2		
1		
Picture	Nonfiction	Fiction

1 : ____ :: more nonfiction than picture books :: 4 : ____

How do you know? _____

2

Bread	1
Meat	6
Fruit	6

____ : Food ::

Squares	4
Circles	7
Triangles	2

: ____

How do you know? _____

3

Blue paint bucket	2
Green paint bucket	7
Yellow paint bucket	5
Red paint bucket	3

5 : ____ :: number of red and blue paint buckets :: 7 : ____

How do you know? _____

Answer Key

Note: There may be more than one correct answer for each analogy. Use judgement when evaluating a student's answers.

Page 6
1. ☺☺☺☺☺; Draw the same number of smiley faces as the number word. 2. 3 + 6 = 9; Write an addition sentence for the number line picture. 3. 19; Write the number pictured by the base-ten blocks.

Page 7
1. 10; Write the number of fish pictured. 2. 13; Write the missing counting number. 3. first; Write the position of the car in line.

Page 8
1. 11; Add one more. 2. 14; Subtract one. 3. 7; Write the number the arrow stopped at.

Page 9
1. 3; Add the groups. 2. 1 ten, 2 ones; Write the number of tens and ones. 3. 4; Write the result of the subtraction problem pictured.

Page 10
1. $\frac{1}{4}$; Write the fraction shown. 2. >; Compare the two numbers. 3. 2; Use a fact family to subtract.

Page 11
1. 30¢; Write the value of the coins. 2. second; Write the missing ordinal number word. 3. 23; Write the number for the tens and ones given.

Page 12
1. 15; Add 3 single-digit numbers. 2. (5¢)(5¢)(5¢)(5¢)(5¢); Draw the equivalent amount using a smaller coin. 3. 17; Count back to write the missing number.

Page 13
1. 45; Add 10. 2. 0; Solve the addition or subtraction problem. 3. $\frac{1}{3}$; Write the fraction for the number of flies to total bugs.

Page 14
1. 2 + 2 + 2; Write the number as a repeated addition of 2. 2. +; Write + or – to make the math sentence true. 3. 70 + 3; Write the tens and ones (expanded form).

Page 15
1. 10; Write the total number of dots shown. 2. 40; Write the number in the middle. 3. (25¢); Draw the single coin with the equivalent value.

Page 16
1. 48 and 68; Write 10 less and 10 more. 2. 2, 4, 6, 8; Count by 2s to count the stars. 3. add 4; Write the number that can be added to make 10.

Page 17
1. ◯; Draw the next shape in the repeating AB pattern. 2. 2 + 6 = 8; Use the commutative property to reverse the addends. 3. 90; Write the next number in the growing (+10) pattern.

Page 18
1. 5 + 2 = 7; Write an addition sentence for the picture. 2. 49; Use the identity property of 0 to add. 3. 12; Count by 2s to write the next number in the growing pattern.

Page 19
1. 5 + 6 = 11; Use the commutative property to reverse the addends. 2. 80; Count by 5s to write the next number in the growing pattern. 3. 5 – 2 = 3; Write the subtraction sentence for the picture.

Page 20
1. ～; Draw the next picture in the repeating pattern. 2. 2; Subtract to write the missing addend. 3. Y; Write the next letter in the repeating pattern.

Page 21
1. ◯; Draw the next circle (or shape) in the pattern. 2. 20; Subtract to write the missing addend. 3. 2; Use a fact family to subtract.

Page 22
1. 70; Subtract to find the missing value. 2. ⚅; Draw the next domino in the pattern. 3. odd; Identify the numbers as even or odd.

Page 23
1. 33; Write the number that should be shaded in the odd-number pattern. 2. money; Classify the items shown. 3. 1 inch; Write the quantitative change in inches shown in the picture.

Page 24
1. 22; Count by 2s to write the next number in the growing pattern. 2. animals; Classify the items shown. 3. less marbles each month; Describe the quantative change shown in the table.

Page 25
1. 16; Write the missing number in the growing (+4) pattern. 2. 2 feet; Write the quantitative change in feet shown in the picture. 3. DDFF; Identify the repeating section of the pattern.

Page 26
1. AABB; Translate the repeating pattern into letters. 2. add 3; Identify the rule for the growing pattern. 3. 8; Use the quantitative information from the table to solve for Rosa's age.

Page 27
1. subtract 5; Identify the rule for the decreasing pattern. 2. 5 – 5; Increase the number subtracted from itself to write the next term in the pattern. 3. 67; Write the number that would be in the center area of the Venn diagram (belonging to both sets).

Page 28
1. ◯; Draw the shape named. 2. 4 corners; Identify the number of corners in the shape named. 3. cube; Write the name of the 3-D figure shown.

Page 29
1. ☐; Draw the shape named.
2. cone; Write the name of the 3-D figure shown. 3. 4 sides; Identify the number of sides in the shape shown.

Page 30
1. circle; Identify the basic shape of the real-world item shown. 2. triangle; Identify the basic shape of the real-world item shown. 3. rectangles; Identify the class of shapes shown.

Page 31
1. ☐; Draw the shape that does not belong in the set. 2. sphere; Identify the basic shape of the real-world item shown. 3. Turn left.; Write the directions described by the picture.

Page 32
1. rectangles; Identify the shapes that make up the faces of the solid figure shown. 2. ☐; Turn the rectangle as was shown with the triangle.
3. 4 equal sides; Identify the number of equal sides in the shape shown.

Page 33
1. ◿; Combine the triangles to make a new shape. 2. △; Identify the shape that does not belong in the set (all others are 3-D). 3. ☐; Draw a shape in the same family as the first but that has all equal sides.

Page 34
1. right; Identify the position of the spider in relation to the leaf. 2. ⊡; Identify one line of symmetry in the shape. Note: Advanced students may draw a vertical and horizontal line of symmetry. 3. ◇; Identify the shape that does not belong in the set.

Page 35
1. ☐☐; Combine the squares to make a new shape. 2. 1 rectangle, 1 square, 2 circles; Identify the combined shapes in the picture.
3. far from home; Describe the distance from home as near or far.

Page 36
1. below star; Describe the position relative to the star as above or below. 2. △; Identify the shape turned in 90°/$\frac{1}{4}$ turn. 3. open figure; Tell whether a figure is open or closed.

Page 37
1. ◯; Use the fold as the line of symmetry to draw the unfolded shape. 2. 9 rectangles; Write the number of rectangles that are formed. 3. ☐; Draw the shape of the face that the two solid figures have in common.

Page 38
1. △☐⬠; Draw the shapes in order of the number of their sides from least to greatest. 2. ▱; Draw a parallelogram that is a reflection of the first parallelogram. 3. triangle; Write the name of the shape that would be pictured if the paper were unfolded.

Page 39
1. 3 paper clips; Measure the item using nonstandard measurement. 2. [7:30]; Write the time described on a digital clock. 3. The cat is taller.; Describe which animal is taller.

Page 40
1. shortest to tallest; Describe the height order of the children. 2. ten o'clock; Write the time shown on the clock. 3. 5 inches; Measure the item to the nearest inch.

Page 41
1. The box is heavier.; Use the scale in the picture to describe which item is heavier. 2. minute hand; Identify the circled hand on the clock. 3. 2 cubes; Measure the item using nonstandard measurement.

Page 42
1. 12 cm; Measure the item to the nearest centimeter. 2. winter; Name the season that comes next.
3. 3 cups; Write the amount shown in the picture.

Page 43
1. 8:30 P.M.; Write the time that is the earliest. 2. greater than; Compare the first capacity to the second capacity. 3. time; Describe what the item measures.

Page 44
1. 9:30 P.M.; Write the time that is the latest. 2. stack of blocks; Identify the picture that is shorter. 3. ruler; Identify the tool that would be used to measure the item shown.

Page 45
1. 12 centimeters; Estimate the length of the beads when 1 bead = 1 centimeter. 2. 4 pounds; Estimate the weight of the books when 1 book = 2 pounds. 3. cups; Identify the measure that does not belong (others measure length).

Page 46
1. A; Identify the ribbon that is longer.
2. 10 grams; Estimate the weight of the paper clips when 1 paper clip = 1 gram. 3. weight; Write what the item measures.

Page 47
1. clam, fish, whale; Use the scales to order the items by weight from least to greatest. 2. D; Identify the rectangle with the larger area.
3. 7 days; Count the number of days that elapse between the circled dates.

Page 48
1. 5 pounds; Estimate the weight of the books when 1 book = 1 pound.
2. about 8 cubes; Estimate the length of the worm in cubes. 3. 1 hour; Write how much time has elapsed.

Page 49
1. about 3 paper clips; Estimate the length of the beads in paper clips.
2. tomorrow; Describe the date based on the first information.
3. 1 hour and 30 minutes; Write how much time has elapsed.

Page 50

1. 𝍷𝍷𝍷 𝍷; Write tally marks to count the number of crayons.
2.

△   𝍷𝍷 ΙΙ
▢   Ι
◯   𝍷𝍷 Ι; Write tally marks in the table to count the number of each shape. 3. 5 marbles; Use the graph to write the number of marbles that Jan has.

Page 51

1. 8 bats; Write the number of bats indicated by the graph. 2. B; Identify the section of the spinner that you would be more likely to land on. 3. 12 party hats; Write the number indicated by the tally marks.

Page 52

1. ▢▢▢▢▢; Draw the number of squares indicated by the graph. 2. 8 eggs; Write the number of eggs indicated by the graph. 3. 27 horses; Write the number indicated by the tally chart.

Page 53

1. ΙΙΙΙ; Make tally marks to count the number of oranges. 2. more; Use the graph to tell whether there are more or less boys. 3. yellow; Identify the section of the spinner that you would be less likely to spin.

Page 54

1. apples; Use the graph to tell which fruit was most popular. 2. 2 snowy days; Use the graph to tell the number of snowy days in December. 3. cats; Use the graph to tell which pet was the most popular.

Page 55

1. Hunter; Use the graph to tell which boy has fewer pencils. 2. swimming and horseback riding; Use the graph to show which two races had the same number of competitors. 3. Friday; Use the graph to tell the day with the least rainfall.

Page 56

1. grade 5; Use the graph to tell which grade has the most number of classes. 2. likely; Write whether the event is likely or unlikely. 3. park; Use the graph to tell which place was most popular.

Page 57

1. 9 coins; Write the total number of data items in the graph. 2. 14 birds; Write the total number of data items in the tally chart. 3. 10 votes; Write the total number of data items in the table.

Page 58

1. the number of students who ride the bus to school; Describe the number based on the table. 2. up 6 degrees; Use the graph to describe the change in temperature from day to day. 3. impossible; Identify whether the event is certain or impossible.

Page 59

1. more paper than cans; Identify the difference between categories on the graph. 2. Toys; Write an appropriate title for the table. 3. pink, yellow, red; Write the items from greatest to least in frequency.

Page 60

1. more picture than fiction books; Identify the difference between categories on the graph. 2. Shapes; Write an appropriate title for the table. 3. number of blue and yellow paint buckets; Write a question about the total of two items from the table.

Notes